Late Autumn, Raking

Late Autumn, Raking

New & Selected Poems

by

Don Kimball

© 2021 Don Kimball. All rights reserved.
This material may not be reproduced in any form, published,
reprinted, recorded, performed, broadcast,
rewritten or redistributed without
the explicit permission of Don Kimball.
All such actions are strictly prohibited by law.

Cover design by Shay Culligan
Cover photo by Ronaldo de Oliveira on Unsplash.com
Author photo by Troy Dondero-Houghton
of Creative Focus Photography

ISBN: 978-1-63980-046-9

Kelsay Books
502 South 1040 East, A-119
American Fork, Utah 84003
Kelsaybooks.com

For my mother, Ruth Deaton Kimball, who dreamed up
those sweet bird-like songs
she used to sing to us at bedtime

Acknowledgments

Many thanks to the editors of the following publications in which some of the poems in this book first appeared, occasionally in slightly different versions:

Alabama Literary Review: "How Frost Met Pound"

Blue Unicorn: "Song for Folding Sheets," "What goes Around Stays the Night"

The Broadkill Review: "Lament," "Ex Nihilo"

The Chimaera: "Prayer for My Father," "Summation"

Dogwood: "The Poet's Worst Nightmare"

Entelechy International: "Winter Song"

First Literary Review-East: "Tall Woman Walking Past a Busker"

The Formalist: "Milk Can"

Garden Lane: "Ursula sleeps upstairs"

Iambs & Trochees: "Birch"

J Journal: "Radio"

Lucid Rhythms: "Jilted"

The Lyric: "Sunday Service," "Cardinals Courting by the Lake," "William, 1949–1966," "For My Son"

The Meeting House: "Knuckle-head"

The Mid-America Poetry Review: "Obstinate Leaves"

Mud Chronicles: "After the Rain"

The Poetry Soup Magazine: "Hipparete, Wife of Alcibiades"

The Poets' Touchstone: "Skipping Stones," "Browsing Used Books," "Salmon"

Quill & Parchment: "When Apple Blossoms Arrive"

The Raintown Review: "Hurricane – September 1938"

Rattle: "Burial for a Stray"

Schuylkill Valley Journal of the Arts: "Deer in a Craft Shop"

Ship of Fools: "Journal of a Flatlander"

Shit Creek Review: "Diary of a Woodsman's Daughter"

Verse Wisconsin: "Farmer's Lament," "Feedback"

Some poems in this book were selected from three chapbooks, **Skipping Stones** (Pudding House Publications, 2008); **Journal of a Flatlander** (Finishing Line Press, 2009); **Tumbling** (Finishing Line Press, 2016).

A number of the above poems and one other ("Passion Reconsidered") have also appeared in anthologies: ***Fashioned Pleasures: Twenty-Four Poets Play Bouts-Rimes with a Shakespearean Sonnet*** (University of Wisconsin Press, 2005); ***The 2008 Poets' Guide to New Hampshire*** (Poetry Society of New Hampshire); ***The 2010 Poets' Guide to New Hampshire: More Places, More Poets*** (the Poetry Society of New Hampshire); ***The Powow River Anthology*** (Ocean Publishing, 2006); ***Poet Showcase: An Anthology of New Hampshire Poets*** (Hobblebush Books, 2015); ***The Powow River Poets Anthology II*** (Able Muse Press, 2020).

I wish to extend my deepest gratitude to Rhina Espaillat, and so many friends and colleagues in the Powow River Poets of Newburyport, MA, with whom I have workshopped many of the poems in this book, and learned what to read, for more than twenty years. Many thanks to you all for your untiring generosity, thoughtful advice and spot-on criticism, as well as your kind support for my efforts. I could not have done this without you!

Contents

From *Skipping Stones* (2008)

Skipping Stones	17
Billet Doux	19
Sunday Service	20
Cardinals Courting by the Lake	21
Deer in a Craft Shop	22
Chair on an Elevator in Oslo	23
The Cousin	24
Signal	25
Obstinate Leaves	26
The Burgher	27
Ursula Sleeps, upstairs…	28
No Need to Call a Taxi	29

From *Journal of a Flatlander* (2009)

Journal of a Flatlander	33
Liam Teething	34
Song for Folding Sheets	35
Passion Reconsidered: *a bout-rimé*	36
Prayer for My Father	37
Diary of the Woodsman's Daughter	39
Milk Can	40
Overbooked	41
The Poet's Worst Nightmare	42
Jilted	44
Hipparete, Wife of Alcabiades	45
Summation	46
Sea Bear	47
Arrhythmia	48
Soldiers of The Great War	49
Hurricane—September 1938	50

What Goes Around Stays the Night	51
How Frost Met Pound	52
Birch	54
William, 1949-1966	55
Winter Song	56

From *Tumbling* (2016)

Making My First Getaway, 1947	59
To See It Go	60
Farmer's Lament	62
Russell Lott or Current Occupant:	63
For My Son	64
Lost and Found	65
Knuckle-Head	67
Flatulent Cows of Rasdorf	68
Full of the Moon	69
If a Tree Falls in The Forest…	70
In The *Cordillera*	71
Park Ranger	72
Keyhole	73
Neighborhood Watch	74
Sonnenizio on a Line From Kim Addonizio	75
Ogie	76
Burial for a Stray	77
Radio	78
Call it My Style	79
Transient Ischemic Attack	80
Contretemps	81
Tumbling	82
Preoccupied	83

New Poems

After the Rain	87
A Stray Norwegian	88
Lament	89
Elegy for a Mannequin	90
Sleep, Wide-Awake	91
Blue	93
Feedback	94
Woman on Ice	95
Late Autumn, Raking	97
New Year's Eve	98
Winter Aurora	100
Ex Nihilo	101
Mirror, Mirror	102
When Apple Blossoms Arrive	103
New Arrival	104
Waking Up	105
Tall Woman Walking Past a Busker	106
Tall Order	107
Short Story	108
After an Overnight Flight, *Your Room Is Almost Ready*	110
The Subwoofer's Denouement	111
Browsing Used Books	112
Salmon	113

From *Skipping Stones* (2008)

Skipping Stones

Best you pick one
burnished

by an ice-age; fit it like
a fine

old fifty-cent
piece

between your forefinger
and thumb;

then, rearing back, pitch it
as though

you're itching to seal the world
record

with a sidearm toss and flick
of the wrist;

letting that flat gray face
leapfrog

across the blue
universe

of a small pond—watching how,
before

it sinks, the stone's repeated
plashing

ripples a drowsy
surface.

Billet Doux

When I'm annoyed
and need you most,

you, my coy
Myrna Loy,

turn, and leave
me shouldering

these padded wings
of a summer jacket—

I, like a toy-
boy loitering

in a gaudy moonlight;
you, not that easy

to kiss. You, *leaving*
me awed by you.

Sunday Service

Looking up
just in time to eye

those long slim legs
waltzing down

the aisle, dressed in black
stylish slacks,

I, like a sly
priest,

quickly bow
my head

in prayer-
like posture, kissed

by the slight
shush of

possibility
passing by.

Cardinals Courting by the Lake

As if they'd shared their vows
and kissed,
the half-masked groom
ruffles his plumage, tilts
his head
to feed his frowsy spouse
crumbs
from
their wedding cake.

Deer in a Craft Shop

It might have been the early morning light
that caught her eye, while she dashed down a one-
way street that night, persuading her to cross
a wide divide—where, later in the day,
she would've had to wobble in the sun
for speeding cars to stop, before she'd dare
to trot the crosswalk. Now, beguiled by some
random need, she strides the four-lane street,
smashing through glitter into shards of glass,
and leaping down, not onto moss or leaves,
but the astonished sales floor. Mouths agape,
the city road crew stand outside to watch,
while the whitetail doe negotiates
a labyrinth of narrow aisles. "Oh, no—
there goes another vase!" yells one of them.
She stops behind a shiny case, as if
gazing with longing at a silver bracelet,
appraising the delicacy of her plight,
when light, that winking light, bewilders her,
invites her back to thrash some inner darkness,
where she attempts to vault a jeweler's bench
and leaps, with a shatter of window panes,
into the blinding glare—a wounded doe
falling two stories to a parking lot,
hobbling a trail of blood and broken vases.

Chair on an Elevator in Oslo

Stationed there,
awaiting scores
of hotel patrons
from a continent of floors,
who cannot stand to wait
for the elevator
to rise
to the occasion, or
get down
to business,
day after day
this cushioned chair,
inviting the weight
of the world,
will not complain,
fall apart
in mute despair
or charge a fare.

The Cousin

She will not seem to see, or maybe care,
how some will hesitate as they approach
the wrought iron tables on the plaza,
not choosing, yet, to sit until they check
which chair she's headed for, an extra chair
the waiter brings to bear the cousin's weight.
During the evening walk she might not mind
that she has fallen behind (her body bent
prematurely), with no devoted dog
to share the space. The laughter, scented flowers,
harbor lights now winking in the distance,
those sighing yachts night-docked along the wharf,
remain aloof from her – the cousin, spinster,
the obligation no one talks about.

Signal

Once a week, the trek
in my pickup truck to play
the dutiful daughter who
puts up with all your picking;
like a servant girl, I hold
your cane (we call it "Junior")
while you haul yourself upon
that seat across from me;
I take you out on jaunts
around the lake, the mountains,
to Sonny's grave just down
the road; read to you,
take you to lunch—and still
it's not enough! Now you're
asking *me* (the atheist)
to take my one day off
and make this drive, again,
to sit with you in church
(as Daddy used to do)
and hear you sigh, once more,
how everyone you know,
Agnes, Mimi and Jo,
has died. Well, Mother dear,
what *are* you waiting for,
a nod, a nudge, another
commandment from The Lord?

Obstinate Leaves

Suppose, at summer's end, the leaves refuse
to fall; our crew-cut grass refuses to fold
or frown. What will Canada geese do,
confused, when they see all nature's run amok?
And how will they fare,
our caravans,
our country fairs,
by Fall's extinction, stalled?

The Burgher

Developer, salesman, stout
merchant in a woolen shirt,
a somber vest,
striding down the narrow sidewalk
of a one-way street,
your shadow
attendant
behind you, now,
carrying on
with the pockmarked face
of an old brick wall,
perhaps reminding you
of all the calls you haven't made—
how time's
limitless landscape
is always
slipping by—while you
(a son, perhaps a father)
precede your shade,
lugging a battered briefcase
as though you've still,
despite this evening's chill,
places to go,
orders to fill.

Ursula Sleeps, upstairs…

        in her late mother's old room,
terminally ill with
        a similar disease;
ready now for the
        final reunion. All her summer hats
put away. In her dreams,
        Aunt Louise rides a quarter horse
at full gallop, racing
        the Boston & Maine along tracks, now
long forgotten, past the Order
        of the Sacred Heart—where blue nuns are prayer-
walking; and a small
        cemetery in back, where her mother lies
in waiting.

No Need to Call a Taxi

When it's time, he stops at your table
and you find you're finished—time to settle.

Whom you know, on this night, is of no
consequence, nor the size of your tip.

Time, now, for the bussing of tables,
and time for weary waiters to end

the evening's languor, to usher us
through the door. No use in unctuous

farewells or haggling. They don't take checks.
No credit cards accepted. It's

strictly cash—and you ought to know.
Time to settle. Time to go.

From *Journal of a Flatlander* (2009)

Journal of a Flatlander

*scribbled
on a three by five
while waiting for the others
to climb down from the tower on Oak Hill*

I am convinced my fear of heights
is more genetic than one likes
to think. As much as others try
I will not be talked out of it,
as much as I would like. My people,
I'm certain, once their boots were tied,
not once lost their slow pace, nor left
the earth until the day they died.
My people, I'm convinced, not being
warriors, explorers, plowed precise
parallel lines behind great teams
of horses; apple-faced farmers, who,
instead of hiking high peaks, which
would dwarf or stymie them, stone-walled
the valleys in between; yet always
proud and sure of foot as mules.
People of some means, yes—though not,
I fear, your people of great heights.

Liam Teething

Soon, your baby teeth will sprout. You'll learn
to bite, to chew, ingest your food; to trust
your mouth to hold this tasty gouda, crust
of bread, but not that broccoli! You'll earn
your parents' true respect. In time, you'll turn,
refuse to swallow what you hate; yet must
you snarl at us for things destined to rust,
erode, despite what pains we take? You'll burn
to speak, to seek the source of a lightning bolt,
wonder what to feed a garden snake
or a wounded bird that falls your prey. The rest,
like 2 + 2 makes 4, you'll learn by rote.
But when your brother knocks you down, you'll ache
for what he did, and soon forgive the pest.

Song for Folding Sheets

Our fingers know: first, you approach me, spare
in scanty underwear, as though you're there
to proposition me. Though I am slow
to hold my end, to fold—in time, I grow
to seize the day. But you, my dear, don't care

to play, for now you're holding up our share—
inviting me to get a clue! I glare,
then make amends—so, back and forth we go;
our fingers know.

After thirty years of marriage wear,
you must admit—I'm not your Fred Astaire;
nor you my Ginger Rogers; but we do-
si-do, a couple's quid pro quo and, lo,
beneath those panties, jockey shorts—I swear
our fingers know!

Passion Reconsidered: *a bout-rimé*

We hurriedly picked a four-room flat just painted,
furnished solely by our youthful passion,
you and I, newly-married, more acquainted
with our bodies than ourselves. The latest fashion
soon lost its early charm for us, as rolling,
rumpled from bed, we met our newborn's gazes.
How foolish I could be, yet still controlling.
The more we age, the more it still amazes,
the girl I chose, a woman you created!
Life gave us notice: grow, or die as doting
lovers, you as well as I – defeated –
had passions overplayed, then left us nothing.
We left behind those maiden rooms of pleasure
that now we gently mock, as well as treasure.

Prayer for My Father

Now let it be cold the night he goes;
let there be snow

which softens the walk, no summer
mosquitoes to swat;

let this be done, so we might hear
their rubber boots

galumph…and be mindful of him,
as men, with care-

worn faces, carry him out. Let him
go, now, in dream's

laborious racket, snoring
in that old house

he fought to keep, where no doctors
will pause to poke

and prod an old man's idling heart;
make evergreens

moan, while they sway in wintry winds;
with branches low

burdened by snow, bow to snuff out
a cold fire. Leave

those blood hounds—howling, when no
master comes round—

howling all night. Let him go out with noise, while there's still time.

Diary of the Woodsman's Daughter

While others clerked in town, our papa worked
the woods in back—yet never yearned for much—
where words, like trees he felled, would simply skirl
as from a horse's mouth ... Axe. A chainsaw,
hammer and maul—not items that a school-
girl has in mind when she first seeks to rhyme
her raw poiesis.
                      I never meant to laugh,
when, meaning to please, our papa mispronounced
the word, and said *po-eet* instead. Oh, how
it echoed, like a mockingbird's lament,
throughout a dark and drafty house, and drove
poor mama further south—that moony noun
our papa mauled. "Po-eet," my brother chirped;
"Po-eet," my sister mocked—Enough! I might
have yelled. Unlearned as papa was, he spoke
a blunt iambic beat until his stroke.

Milk Can

As if she's heard intruders at the door,
but would not trust the lock to keep her safe,
should they come bursting in—who knows what for—
the widow, clutching at her flannel robe,
takes hold of an old milk can—like her kitchen,
a handy catch-all; this object that cannot
object to her unladylike abuse—
tilts it back and slowly wheels it sideways
(as she once saw her husband deal with barrels),
steers it through a narrow passageway,
between a closet, some unforgiving stairs,
clear to the entry, where she lets it go,
wedges it tight against the door, says, *There!*—
as if she's finally got that big old house,
with all its rooms, secured against desire;
as if, by blocking doors, she's doused the fire.

Overbooked

Often I find that where I take a book
out of my bookcase—Plato, Proust, Plotinus,
some epic I ought to read—another tome
leans in to take its place. My bookish pride
gets pushed aside by other books I've bought;
still sprouting Post-its, like disheveled hair,
books do what books are bound to do, they claim
their dusty lairs. And while my appetite
for buying more provokes my wife, books plot
on either side, prepare to slap a lien
on the vacant spot, until I shove
into place a new-bought book; those daunting stacks
I sought to read—now, age-old hardbound bores—
still hang around, displaced, on couch or floor,
demand I read or tote them out the door.

The Poet's Worst Nightmare

His wristwatch dies; his printer jams
beyond repair; his flatscreen gets

the blues. He receives not one,
but two rejection slips—for the same

three poems he submitted not
six days ago. A paraplegic,

stalking him in a wheelchair,
claims he plagiarized her prized

poem. His flight to NYC,
where he's receiving the Pulitzer Prize,

is cancelled. At a reading, some scowl,
others heckle. Critics pan

his latest poems: his rhyming is in-
exact; his lines, excessively

enjambed, sprout anapests
like weeds. The Borders crowd dismisses

his formal verse as maladroit,
a throwback, a curse; at Biker Joe's,

his poetry pals recoil when he
assumes the guise of Edward Purvis

strumming a ukulele, as he
recites his anguished Alcaics. He grows

despondent, and tries to shoot himself;
instead he nicks his neighbor's cat.

For the 180th time,
he mails his manuscript, his *oeuvre;*

his publisher declares bankruptcy, sells
insurance instead. The poet downs

a few too many Mai Tais with
his rival and forgets to go

to his radio interview. Oprah
finds the poet's memoir, now in

its fourth reprint, a hoax. To make
amends, he composes his long-awaited

Summa Theologica
in blank verse, but discovers God

has fled the scene; Jesus Christ
and Mary Magdalene have eloped.

His mother leaves him a message, "Honey?
I've baked you a pecan pie!" His wife

leaves him for Robert Bly; his lover
concedes she loves her husband. His son

hates to read.

Jilted

How hard I hurt, through April, May and June
to thrash this out in verse, work out the stress,
buffooned by the mean light of an old moon,
awake, alone, at home where I'd obsess,
replaying what Bo did and why—that snake
who left me by the altar, love all moot;
lonely for friends to bring me carrot cake,
to make me laugh and help me cuss that beaut!
Then, I put on my face, this mask; like Garbo
I needed solitude, to cut and play
the blues; to moan a ballad like those hobo
poets, Whitman, Villon—and end the day,
not high or drunk, nor one who twangs a rhinestone
guitar; I bawled, then flushed his cheap cologne.

Hipparete, Wife of Alcabiades

Let's say you are an ill-starred general's wife,
your father's gift to Alcibiades.
You bear his son, his heart. Or so you thought.
His concubine (expecting!) shares your house.
But then you try to leave it all behind.
You're desperate, though, for him to ache for you.
Distracted by his prize, his fame, your husband
cultivates his guise, seems not to notice.
Your older brother, whom you sought for help,
not willing to embarrass Athens' hero,
sends you back to your husband, where you have
no voice. Wouldn't you, in this woman's place,
without Medea's god machine to aid,
seek death's embrace—or pierce him with his blade?

Summation

Some things occur for no good reason. Take this:
after years of absence, your only child comes home.
He's there in the darkness where he's always been,
and as you step inside the doorway, see
his shadow bounding toward you, it's easy to
mistake him for a stranger, a man
with rape on his mind; and since you're packing
what's meant to give you that needed edge
to deal with threats of mayhem—which,
since Cain and Abel, bedevil men and women—
you reach for it and use it, as you've learned
from months of practice. Now, instead
of bottles, cans, those outlines of a man
coming toward you on the shooting range,
this outline of your son
on the kitchen floor.

Sea Bear

With snowshoe paws she sweeps the snow
sniffing blubber beneath the floe.
Her canines primed to seize and tear,
blood smears her incandescent hair.
Where arctic hunger binds them all,
she yanks her meal, bites the small
scruff, then shucks the skin and eats
the steaming fat. The ice retreats.

Arrhythmia

Your breast is beating out of tune.
Your face reflects an ashen moon.
Your body flags, a sudden chill,
As of the prey before the kill.

Soldiers of The Great War

I. Verdun, 1916

Your government has fled the city,
the G.Q.G. is uninspired,
and all you want to do is die.
If Big Bertha doesn't kill you first
your sergeant will (if you desert);
reveillez-vous, soldat garcon,
remember Sedan, hold Verdun!

That mediocre Moltke's blitz
(von Schlieffen's final words forgotten),
Gott bewahre, you get the shits!
If a poilu doesn't kill you first
your sergeant will (if you desert);
so, mind your *schwere geschütze, mein junge,*
storm Mort Homme, smash Verdun!

II. The Somme

Your brother's dead at 21,
and all you want to do is run,
instead you're sent to kill the Hun.
If a sapper doesn't blast you first,
the sergeant will (if you refuse);
so, over the top, Tommy, boy,
it's up the ladder, rung by rung!

Hurricane—September 1938

The absence of gulls, those cirrus clouds, the sea
a yellow-green...all the signs were there,
but hurricanes did not come up this far,
our minds preoccupied by winds of war.
                                        —My Father

This wasn't just another three-day blow
you'd grown up with, not this increasing bellow.
A sultry haze incites the whirling Cyclops;
fixing its sky blue eye, it leaves no place
to hide. Although you rush to block your doors,
your picture windows—it's no use—the mounting
surf, now a herd of raging elephants,
will find a way to dash your homes, your dreams;
swells pounding at New England's cement seawalls
(jarring seismographs as far away
as icy Fairbanks), swamping buses, yachts
and trains; waves, breaking higher than a house,
bursting through windows, flimsy walls and doors,
as though it must devour you, shoving chairs
and tables apart, to chase you, floor to floor,
until you find your heart can stand no more.

What Goes Around Stays the Night

For Rhina P. Espaillat

A most peculiar dame! I like the way
she rhymes—the last line rhyming with the first;
like Echo, how she struts and makes us thrilled
to risk, to take that turn we learn to weigh;
casting her couplets elsewhere, a thought rehearsed,
we hear somewhere within the heart; we end
where we begin, with more than we intend;
an unexpected twist, a boomerang—
when used to hearing voltas Shakespeare willed
to us; more *vida* than village rapper's slang;
which is to say—what goes around, will stay
to bite, to nettle or tickle in delight
with deeper understanding of the night,
as well as how our words may ricochet.

How Frost Met Pound

   —a found poem from a paragraph by Jeffrey Meyers
   in his biography of Robert Frost

Once Flint told Pound about our Frost
being in town,

why Pound invited him to stop
by Number 10

Church Walk, in Kensington; the fox
sending him

that dodgy red Ezraic card
which said, "At home,

sometimes." Now, Frost, provoked by Pound's
impertinence,

was not about to drop by until
his firstborn book

A Boy's Will had come out. So, late
that following March,

1913, this barn-sour bard
from north of Boston

found himself, at thirty-nine,
sounding out

a beaten path, hedge-rowed between
gothic steeple

and burial mounds, then made to wait
while the renowned

impresario towels off
his famous flaunt

of ferruginous hair, Frost knocking on
Pound's door.

Birch

Now, burdened by the drag of heavy snow
grasping its gaunt old trunk, my birch must go.
Where once it stood amid an isle of flowers,
it stoops alone, unbraced against snow showers.
This statesman, in a compromised position,
cannot be propped or saved, has no ambition
except to bend the rules and block the way
while we the people plot an arbor day.
Old American Gray, you haven't a prayer;
the end of a long, unhappy love affair!
As I apply my chainsaw's jagged smile,
reducing you to slash, a punk wood pile—
birches beware: you're bound to lose your place
to Japanese Maple, or a parking space.

William, 1949-1966

On Sunday morning you will drown,
fate tossing us four instead of five:
the task, so early in our lives,
to dredge the depths of life foreshortened.
What author worth his name, unless
it only be his first attempt,
and he, some minor deity
still incomplete—like you and me—
could write you off in Chapter One.
Yes, you, who must have seemed the best,
the brightest, proud protagonist!
A bitter tale, in which you're dead:
the book I wish I'd never read.

Winter Song

I see an arctic lake
below my window,
some great white whale
articulated by
winter's dying light.
But I know
it can't be so; there is
no arctic swell
this far south,
just an old man's North
Pole overheated;
my neighbor's acre pond
all frozen over;
no fishy smell of salt,
except what salt
a prudent man applies
to black ice on asphalt;
no scattered rocks
or seashells
to scallop an icy shore. None
of that bony flotsam
to glean. Still, I dream
an arctic sea,
enticing me, beyond
these barren trees,
the sweep of arctic winds
and heaps of frozen snow.

From *Tumbling* (2016)

Making My First Getaway, 1947

Awake for three days
with my cries,
you tied my waist
to a gray rock,
half my size.

I'd seen Dad
grab a rock
and plumb a fence post
or block the car
from rolling backward
down the driveway. I
yanked my rock
through alders and mud,
halfway into town

before you got
the call
from Mrs. Potts
who'd spotted cars
swerving and
your little boy
along the asphalt,
leaning against the anchor
of that rock.

To See It Go

For MK

Odd to see the big old house
with its portico, still there
on top of the hill
like a grand hotel
or landlocked liner.

Easier, perhaps,
to see it go—our house,
skirted by azaleas,
lilacs and rhododendrons
our grandmother planted,
the pond we skated on,
the apple orchard, fields
and woods I roamed—
if, instead, another family
like ours
filling all 14 rooms
with their foibles
and fuss;
someone, like our father,
seeing the lawns get mowed,
replacing shingles, window panes,
scraping, repainting clapboards,
before the house goes

the way the barn went,
both ends leaning inward
like folding hands,
collapsing
one day
in a clatter
of dust,

a cellar hole
rimmed by snow.

Farmer's Lament

She milked the cow,
I rode the plow;

She planted seeds,
I pulled the weeds;

She birthed the lambs,
I sheared the rams;

She cleaned our house,
I hunted grouse.

Then, Christmas Day,
Tending the sow,
She passed away.

I'm selling now.

Russell Lott or Current Occupant:

Not to worry;
wherever you are,
ensnared in some far-off plot
or well-off
in witness protection,
we still consider you
one of us.

For My Son

I kneel before you,
as a mother might,
to button your shirt
or tie a shoe,
my son, alert, subdued,
your first train ride

away from home, I could
not hide my tears from you.
The fleeting bullet of a
train leaves me muddled
in this joyless dream,
on a crowded platform,
still conceiving you;
a son I never knew.

Lost and Found

For PEK

Washing my hands, love,
I found your earring,
and wondered why
it was in *my* sink,
instead of yours,
stuck between
the pop-up stopper
and the collerette.
It held on
for nearly 24 hours,
without either of us
spotting it.

Amazing it wasn't tossed
by a cat's paw
or lost
in water
blasting out
of the faucet's
small Niagara,
shoving it past
the hair-clotted tailpiece
to disappear
somewhere
in the maze
of plumbing.

How attached it must be
to your lovely earlobe,
your silver earring, still
dangling
its dainty
hexagonal shield

embossed by
tiny colored stones,
the clasp
grasping!

Knuckle-Head

Hijacking
my work
by whacking

his bill
at the roof
of my neighbor's shiny
Cadillac,

the sapsucker's
ruckus
rattles
a battle with pot
and spoon;

its rat-a-tat-tat
a brassy dit-dit-dot
to tag
his territory or
tattoo
a lover's plot.

Flatulent Cows of Rasdorf

It was sparked
by static electricity
from the swishing cow brush
of a massaging machine.
Inside the dairy barn,
which housed ninety cows,
a methane cloud
had been swelling
all week.

Nearly a mile off
we saw
the eerie flash
of flames,
a fiery cypress,
or was it Odin's torch?

According to the *polizei,*
one cow
was treated for minor burns.

Full of the Moon

What do you do when the sun
has lost his place and the moon's
full of herself? That carnival face
troubling the night, her gauzy
luminous glare behind tree limbs
black as guns. Cache your cakes
of honey, there is no place
to hide
except inside,
away from all the windows;
still, you know she's there!

If a Tree Falls in The Forest…

While honeybees hum in noon heat
trees prefer to sit it out
on a granite rock
and talk,
or stretch out across the grass for a midday snooze,
exposing their girth.

At desks, in a classroom, you will not hear
the rustle of their leaves,
limbs gesturing,
as they go on
about forest fires, frost cracks, Dutch Elm, men
with power saws.

Younger trees in need of pruning
lie next to each other, crooning
like lovers lolling on the green; if you
step outside, you might
catch them in a flurry of limbs
going at it,
one birch
on top another.

        They'll rise, again,
when birds begin their gleaning
in the cool of the late afternoon,
or if a Monarch Tree
sees you lumbering
over the horizon and,
like a crow,
creaks out a clarion call.

In The *Cordillera*

Under the muddy
tumble of mountain-torrents,
a clatter of stones.

Clop, clop, clop of hooves
across rocks, sea shells, lava.
Sunlight slips away

from the cratered face
of this earth. Deep in cold dark
old stones rattle on.

Park Ranger

> "...thousands of migrating lady beetles, an endless swarm of them, undulating..."
> —Jordan Fisher Smith, Nature Noir

Warm, dry and dusty,
the wind picks up, rumbling in
your ears. An amber

haze billows between
you and the scattered birch trees
beyond the cobbled

beach. Hobbling on
pebbles, you step inside this
burnished cloud: a mass

migration of wings,
these lucky lady beetles
almost endlessly

swarm, undulating
up the canyon on the wind.
One by one, they tick

your stiff, broad brimmed hat;
landing on your shirt, crawling
on your sleeves. You turn,

facing these tiny
migrants, do you feel them flow
over you slowly?

Autumn's afternoon
sun glowing through a million
wings like saffron robes.

Keyhole

The late
afternoon light,
a keyhole in mauve clouds,
highlights the sheets of yesterday's
scant snow.

Neighborhood Watch

Aroused
by a cacophony
of curses,
supposing crows
are on to something—
an owl, a fox, a hawk—
I haul out of bed
and, lurching
toward the crack of dawn,
all its racket,
steal across the lawn
toward a stand of cedars
behind my neighbor's house.

Barely feeling the dew
on my toes, I catch
a murder
of crows,
in the cocklight,
mobbing
what looks
like a red-tailed hawk,
when I spot
the widow's face,
pressed against her bedroom window,
eyeing me.

Sonnenizio on a Line From Kim Addonizio

What happened, happened once. So now it's best
we leave, forget it happened. It's for the best;
it only happened just this once, okay?
Why it happened is of no consequence…
mere happenstance. Don't think too much of this,
it'll leave you unhappy…only happened once.
I'll say, "it never happened," the humping part,
and let my hapless wife assume we kissed
just once, a mishap of one too many bourbons.
It happens. Let me excuse myself, and please
keep it quiet, okay? So it happened—
the back end slap, a bit of tickle, best
that you and I forget this happened; now leave,
it just so happens she's nuts; but not naïve.

Ogie

It's Sunday morning, and the lawn's unmowed;
neighbor dogs are barking. Ron is tying
his tie, Irene slips on her summer dress
when their willful, half-grown Westie takes off
tailing a trailer-load of jet skis towed
behind a pickup. Only yesterday,
a neighbor caught him chasing off a bear!
The dog just keeps on going; did Irene –
or maybe Ron—forget to turn it on,
that invisible fence? In Sunday clothes
they rush along the street, those steeple bells
beseeching them to hurry up. It's such
a busy road between the towns. Now Ron,
tieless and gasping, there before Irene;
cars slowing down, swerving, driving on.

Burial for a Stray

For BB

Two dogs and a cat who knew you best
came by and sat as I dug a hole.
Azaleas bloom there where you rest.
Two dogs, a cat, who knew you best,
keep vigil here: at whose behest?
Torn ear, one eye: life takes its toll.
Two dogs and a cat who knew you best
came by and sat. I dug the hole.

Radio

What should I do, my love,
when you—nearly twenty years
younger—fly off into the night
pursuing the guy who smashed the rear
window of our new car—what
but reach for that
baseball bat
gathering dust
behind the cellar door?

Suppose you get to him
while I'm still lagging behind,
gasping, and he goads
you into stabbing him
with that greasy steak knife
you grabbed
from the kitchen table
on your way out of the house;
or worse,

when he's unable to pry that thing
loose with his screwdriver
and he's got no use
for his bleeding hand,
another woman
complicating his life,
he turns to you?

Call it My Style

When my wife yells at me,
or calls me a name in derision,
I smile
to avoid a collision.

When my smartass neighbor,
with his bloviations,
tempts me to reconstruct him, I
decline all invitations.

When my mother blurts out, "Don't worry, dear,
you'll get by on charm,"
I thank her for the compliment.
Maybe she means no harm.

When the man she calls my father,
sneers his dissatisfaction,
Sorry, I say.
That's my reaction.

Perhaps walking away
is in my DNA.

Transient Ischemic Attack

Today, after 60 years,
my brain abandoned my right arm
still holding my wallet
high above the counter
as if to signal
for silence
or a waiter.

I glared at my hand, as if
reduced to a relic,

"Put the wallet on the counter!"

My left arm, servant,
supporting actor, brother
buckled my seatbelt
and drove me
to Emergency.

Contretemps

Her fifty-seventh
slips by;

three days later,
she cries

*you never even said
a word.*

He tries to dash off
a card

to slip beside her favorite
Pinot

when she comes home
from work,

but his nervous tremor, that Richter scale
of age,

turns all his sentiments
to scribbles;

he types a love letter
in Papyrus font,

lays out old photographs to prop
an evening;

reaching for them, she spills
the wine.

Tumbling

down
those cellar stairs
I knew so well,
fumbling, reaching for
what is
not there;

I tried to keep
an open mind,
not waste this moment
brooding on
what I was
leaving
behind…

except, on the tile floor,
my body stopped,
my elbow, my knees, my shoulder
just couldn't wait
to show me
how I'd dropped,
that much older.

Preoccupied

Lately, I've been
lapsing.
Intending to stash
a dirty serving dish
in our dishwasher, I
pull out the drawer
of silverware instead.

No matter.

Just the other night,
holding an empty platter
amid a lot of chit-chat
and clatter of plates,
I find myself
pulling open yet
another drawer, this one
housing all the trash;
I circumnavigate
the house like
a fool on a blind date.

No matter.

If someone asked,
I'm apt to say,
just another poem
I'm working on today.

New Poems

After the Rain

The tiny drop,
a diamond stud
on a green leaf,

the sting
of sunlight,
beseeching.

Adirondack chair,
a phoebe chirping,
pidiweew, pidireep,

but oh, the spastic chattering
of a cat
behind that feeble screen.

A Stray Norwegian

He still comes back, we're sure of that,
the *skogkatt* who adopted us for five years,

though we will not see him, this morning,
looking like a rag mop dampened by dew,

ambling up the long winding back porch stairs
like a crippled saint or beggar

we haven't the heart to turn away;
rising out of the high cooling spears

beneath the Japanese Crab Apple,
assuming his haunting shadowy posture,

the face you and I think we see
in passing the kitchen window,

until we throw open the door;
until we grieve and let him go.

Lament

Pity the saber-tooth cat
last seen with its spotted coat
during the late Pleistocene—
its curved canines, the size of
white bananas, piercing deep
into the neck of a sloth
once big as the bison or
a wooly mammoth; that free,
and seemingly easy snack
half-submerged in coal-tar seep,
only to be trapped with its
prey, then 10,000 years out
deemed an artifact of fate.

Pity the lion, both ears
riddled with bullet holes;
his lanky belly laid out
in dry grass, disemboweled
by a half-tusked, waggling
warthog protecting her piglets.

Pity, too, our barnyard cat,
half his mouth bitten off one
morning, by a cornered rat,
bagged by a farmer and tossed
into the Merrimack. Rings
widening in the water,
a drooling cat's epitaph.

Pity them all except the rat.

Elegy for a Mannequin

You do not blink
or breathe
or even flinch
when a mosquito
tries your bloodless cheek.

Your face affects that futile,
fashionable smile,
until one day
the buildings,
like tall trees
in a stiff breeze,
begin to sway.

You leap
before our eyes,
shaking your blue chiffon—
chic ingénue! —
until you're cast
down from your pedestal—
alive at last.

Sleep, Wide-Awake

When Sleep stays up
for the late-night shows,

her long blond hair
gone to weeds,

mocking Wall Street bozos
yawping like crows
on her wall-sized TV;

When Sleep sees Night
folding into Day,
with Theia's glare
upcasting the shades,
decreeing her (Sleep)

a castaway

rolling off the couch
to squirrel herself
away

inside a sleeping bag,
on the cold basement floor;

When Sleep's raccoon eyes
are stinging,
squinting deep into the stygian darkness

of yet another four,
five, or six
in the morning;

When Sleep's sudden shiver
hauls her up,
recalling,

what seems like only yesterday,
that final exam at Old Main,

her rumpled PJs
casting a pall
over the crowded study hall
as she's stumbling in,
falling
into a desk chair;

When Sleep tweets her sister Claire,
I can't keep doing this!

bingeing a box of fried clams,
milk shakes, day-old pastries;

When Sleep burps
a record-breaking burp,

and eats her Prius for dessert,

leaving the rubber wheels,
like crumbs on a plate,

hawking,

then feeling a seismic grumble
in her stomach;

When Sleep hurls up the night

Blue

Ambien's not the fix.

Nix that strain of bright blue lights,
flat screen, iPhone, tablet, laptop,

eyes transfixed
stealing your sleep,

getting you blue,
heavy-lidded,

paddling
daylong along the River Styx.

Ambien's not the fix.

Consider this, instead:
a soothing shower, slide into bed,
picture a parade of elephants
lumbering across the savannah;
a mesmerizing murmuration of starlings
confiding in the darkening sky;
a school of dolphins
leaping side-by-side,
surfing the sunlit tide.

Feedback

For AL

One night, my son-in-law, the therapist,
opined I "over-think" things. I didn't think
to ask him what he meant; nor did I shoot him
a snappy comeback. Stayed up all that night
and thought and thought and thought some more; as light
arranged the room, decided my son-in-law,
rude as he might be, had got that right.
I might delete a word, then bring it back.
I brood, I ruminate on what he takes
for granted—good and evil, light and shadow,
subtle nuances in the nebulae.
I almost kissed the man for what he said,
but, thinking it over, wrote this poem instead.

Woman on Ice

For BA

Cleaning one of the lakefront houses,
she eyes her husband slowly driving by;
imagines slipping into cold water
and letting go.

Then she hears the dogs.
She kicks off the vacuum,
cocks her head.
Something in their yelping
draws her to the bay window
overlooking a lake of ice.

A dog, she sees, up to its ears
in icy water,
front paws padding
at sheets of ice
giving way beneath him.
Another scooches close
to the fractured edge,
giving him
an occasional lick
on the nose.

Pulling on a sweater
she bounds down the back steps
towards the beach.

Cold air nips her face,
as she straddles
a neighbor's ladder,
crawls
from rung to rung,
out towards the pair.

Rebuffed, the second dog
nips at her.
She manages to grab the first
by his scruff and yanks him, sopping wet
and shivering, out of the lake
and back to the bank.

"Wait, whose mutt is it?" She yells.

The neighbor, walking away
with his ladder, shrugs his shoulders.

Cradled in her burly arms,
she carries the dog home
and keeps it—the only pet
she ever had.

Until one night, during a fight
with her husband,
the dog leaps
and bites the fist
usually
meant for her.

Late Autumn, Raking

As sunlight falls
behind the trees,
a brumal wind
battles all
the browned-out leaves,
winding them up
for a fall.

At break of day,
the dead leaves
a tattered bed,
I rake them all
into smoldering heaps,
wheezing
while I claw
those harried stragglers,
hissing
from under window sills;
skittering
like mice along
the pocked foundation;
or lying low
between the knurled toes
of an old oak.

By nightfall,
the sidewalk
swells with sheaves,
demanding
all these leaves
recall
where they belong.

New Year's Eve

For HF

With a bowl of salad
your offering,
you hurried toward the dining table
hastily set for the six of us
(our dinner delayed by a frozen pipe).

But oh, you didn't see
that dishwasher door
one of us had left open.

Your long legs
had pedaled countless miles,
but now they met an impediment
none of us foresaw.

The bowl flew out of your hands,
cherry tomatoes, lettuce, shredded carrots
spattered the kitchen floor
like scraps from a crappy year.

Your hands reached out,
but found nothing at all,
not even
one of us—
to break your fall.

What else could you do
when you hit the hardwood floor,
shattering your right elbow?

Your arm confined
to a pillow in your lap,
you had to scrap your cycling tour—

the dream of wheeling
in Amsterdam—
face the new year

with surgical pins,
the plate implant,
a cast,
PT,

a year spent healing!

Winter Aurora

That tangle of alders
haloed in bluish-gray

behind us,
where nothing breathes

or moves,
fixed in an eerie nimbus

highlighting
implausible limbs

purified
by a soft rime,

crystalline
spangles or
prisms

dangling
from a chandelier—until

a dazzle
of sunlight

diamonds the thin
limbs.

Ex Nihilo

inspired by Carlo Rovelli's Seven Brief Lessons on Physics

A dot,
so dense, so hot,
it shot in all directions—space

fat with matter, time and energy,
in no time flat
inflating that starless extremity

like a bell-shaped balloon
with a ghostly afterglow.
Was it luck or by design

this sublime, forever-
expanding evening sky in time
spurred, like a burst of fireworks,

billions of galaxies
wheeling like whirligigs—each one
spangling hundreds of billions

of suns such as our own? This
swirling universe undulating;
at times, so agitated

some bleeding star
yawns a hole
too deep for us to plumb.

Mirror, Mirror

Some long
lost twin,

my vis-à-vis
opposite me,

seeing eye
to eye; how

complementary
she and I.

When Apple Blossoms Arrive

I like to hide for hours
in the shade
of trees

heeding the hum
of bumblebees

bumping, bumping

buzzed
like drunken dandies
on a nectar spree;

fat, clumsy bumblers
clad in fuzzy black
orange and yellow fur coats.

This bumper crop of bees
bothers neither cows, nor goats,
nor you and me.

See how
they've multiplied!

Hard at work
to provide, provide.

New Arrival

For NEF

She sought me out night and day,
while I was trying to write,
with her stubborn quirks and fears;
her little drawings, scribbled
notes she slid beneath the door.

At last I put down my pen,
picked up the long-stemmed flower
she drew me. A gift, perhaps
a sign we're blending!
                       Although,
for a moment her drawing
drew me back to a dark time,
my little brother's lifeless
body under the water.

Snow smothered the window sill,
my car, the driveway, as I
dredged her drawings for signs.
Did this little girl feel safe?
Her still-embittered mother
didn't—and remained haunted
by dreams of her own father.

By summer, she found a friend,
the two of them hopscotching
along a patch of sidewalk
they chalked in a latticework
of boxes, the little girl—
more than forty years ago—
I came to call my daughter.

Waking Up

In a dream I did not mean to dream,
I see my wife—or so it seems—
leaning against a younger man
in the shadow of a willow tree,
his beard, his shaggy head of hair
silhouetted
in the early morning's glare,
her lovely lips, like kissing cherries,
pressing his!

I clench my hands and feel
a burning in my chest.
                          How pleased
I am to snap awake,
escaping all the disarray
of dream's demented life,
to feel my wife
of many nights
and days,
lying next to me,
dreaming.

Tall Woman Walking Past a Busker

You almost feel
the saxophone's appeal,

as her shimmering dress,
a small waterfall,

caresses
her long, long legs.

Tall Order

For ML

Think tall, granddaughter, even though
you rise all of five feet, hauling out
your plastic stool on the heels of that
statuesque PhD in leopard pumps,
to see over the podium. Pause,
claim your poise;
scan our faces;
let your words reverberate
around the rotunda.

Short Story

You plop in front of me
inside

the crowded theater;
you stop

then carry on in front of us
at our favorite
concert,

your boundless back, abundant head
a total eclipse

of the main attraction.

Outstretched arms and fingers
achieving

the higher elevations of
basketball

jump shots; top shelves
of Home Depot

or Shop-N-Save; not to mention—
all that

added work you strapped
me with,

grasping at rungs of
a ladder,

replacing plastic smoke
alarms,

light bulbs, your oblong nob
clobbered

when you couldn't be bothered
to bend

or stoop, while bounding
through

that dimly-lit Purple Pit.
I might

even be pleased (in my own
small way)

to see you humbled when
you stumble

on a tall doorsill and fall,
except

for all that carpet space
you'd seize,

a stiff
the size of Tennessee.

After an Overnight Flight, *Your Room Is Almost Ready*

Sprawled
on a chaise lounge,
only the murmur
of lake water
lapping at sand,
you utter
a vagabond's
long drawn-out yawn,
supplanted by
a stertorous sigh;
eyes
heavy-lidded,
longing for the elusive
snooze
with central air,
a goose
down pillow
to place
your face
on.

The Subwoofer's Denouement

Several times you give it a whack,
that big black box (an old Best Buy!)
plunked behind a lackluster Lazy-Boy
still woofing, woofing,

You fiddle with dials
(symbols barely legible),
but it won't stop woofing;

Why did I buy this crap device?

You unplug it,
count to 30,
then plug it in, again,

that woofalaggin grunting on and on,
a gorilla in your woofbox
trying to break out—only now
it's after midnight,
someone's banging on your door,
"Hey, shut the fuck up!"
and you're stuck,
despite the long commute,
bootstrapping shit
jobs, college loans,
a rainy-day start-up,
trying to reboot
a piece of junk
in a seedy Airbnb
in Kissimmee!

Browsing Used Books

pages blessed
by arrows, ticks
or check-marks,
wagging their tiny tails
at striking lines;

annotations,
like homilies,
anointing the margins; and then,

the table of contents,
a marquee
of featured lyrics,

an evening sky
studded by
asterisks.

Salmon

For PM

Fed by the twin rivers,
Pemigewasset, Winnipesaukee,
you are the river
the first people called
Merrimac; and I,
your saw-toothed salmon, still
nosing
tiny fiords
of the northern stream
white immigrants cleaned.

Come spring,
the Merrimac—my old haunt,
my mainstay—is flashing its teeth
from Franklin Falls,
where tributaries meet,
down past the rapids
of Amoskeag Falls, shadowed
by reflections of old bricks,
to the ocean
they call The Atlantic.

Do not forget me, river,
when, leaping
upstream to lay my roe,
I strike the rocks,
to try to cut the line
that moving shadow heaved,

hooking my lip.

About the Author

Don Kimball is the author of three chapbooks, *Tumbling* (Finishing Line Press 2016), *Journal of a Flatlander* (Finishing Line Press 2009) and *Skipping Stones* (Pudding House Publications 2008). Don's poetry has appeared in *The Blue Unicorn, The Lyric, Rattle, The Raintown Review, Shit Creek Review, Ship of Fools* and numerous other journals and anthologies. A retired family therapist, Don is the recent past president of the Poetry Society of New Hampshire (2014 – 2020), and a longstanding member of the Powow River Poets in Newburyport, MA.

www.ingramcontent.com/pod-product-compliance
Lightning Source LLC
Chambersburg PA
CBHW032235080426
42735CB00008B/868